RESPONDING to LITERATURE 3–6

Activities That Build Confident Readers and Writers

Written by
June Hetzel

Contributions by Heather Phillips, Jenifer MacLowry,
Marsha Bowser, and Sergio Perez

D1402618

Editor: Sheri Samoiloff
Illustrator: Jenny Campbell
Cover Illustrator: Karl Edwards
Designer: Moonhee Pak
Cover Designer: Moonhee Pak
Art Director: Tom Cochrane
Project Director: Carolea Williams

© 2002 Creative Teaching Press, Inc., Huntington Beach, CA 92649
Reproduction of activities in any manner for use in the classroom and not for commercial sale is permissible.
Reproduction of these materials for an entire school or for a school system is strictly prohibited.

Table of Contents

Introduction

Responding to Literature 3–6 is a collection of classroom-tested teaching strategies and student activities that promote reading and generate literature responses in numerous formats. This resource is comprised of meaningful and motivating activities that are easily adaptable to any literature selection.

Each activity is presented with the intent of expanding students' reading and comprehension skills. Questions and activities encourage higher-level thinking, develop students' decision-making and evaluative skills, and simultaneously develop their fluency in reading and writing.

Research has confirmed that the more students read, the better they read; and the more they read familiar text, the more automatically they recognize words. The more automatically students recognize words, the more fluently they read. The more fluent students become, the more expressive and confident they are in their reading. And so goes the reading cycle for successful readers!

The exciting independent reading strategies and literature response activities in *Responding to Literature 3–6* make it easy for your students to read text and interact with the book selection. This book includes

- ready-to-use reproducibles
- step-by-step directions for working with your students on various literature selections
- rationale for developing the skills presented
- ideas for extending each activity

This resource provides students with the opportunity to embark on the journey of reading and the pleasure that comes along with it.

Getting Started

Responding to Literature 3–6 contains numerous activities, in various exciting formats, to stimulate students' thinking and understanding of key vocabulary and basic story elements such as characterization, comparisons, setting, story sequence, and plot summary.

This book is divided into two sections. The first section presents independent reading strategies to build reading fluency and comprehension. The second section features literature response activities to strengthen comprehension. The activities are very flexible and can be revisited throughout the year. Choose the activities that work best with your students.

Independent Reading Strategies

The Independent Reading Strategies section (see pages 5–9) presents fun, stimulating ways to encourage reading. Use these strategies to have students read poems, novels, articles, and trade books.

Literature Response Activities

The Literature Response Activities section (see pages 10–63) includes a variety of teaching strategies and time-saving reproducibles. First, decide how you would like students to read the selection (e.g., independent reading, shared reading, or guided reading). Then, choose an activity, and copy a class set of the corresponding reproducible.

To ensure student success, it is important to model for students how to complete the activities in this resource before having them work independently. For example, photocopy an activity reproducible and enlarge it to chart size, or create a transparency of the reproducible. In a whole-group setting, lead the class step-by-step through the process indicated in the directions, always modeling your thinking about the process using the "think-aloud" procedure so students are cognizant of your every thought and action regarding the process from reading the story, to thinking about the story, to actually recording your response on the reproducible.

Finding Patterns

Purpose

Use this activity to help students recognize specific elements or characteristics of a story. When readers identify elements or characteristics of a story, they are able to locate information more quickly and understand the piece better.

Procedure

Select a short piece of fiction or nonfiction from a specific genre (e.g., mystery, fairy tale, historical fiction, biography, how-to, cause and effect). Brainstorm with students what they already know about the genre. For example, for a biography, students may say that it contains information about a person's life, including his or her accomplishments, contributions to society, early life, education, date of birth, and date of death (if deceased). Have students read the story and record the elements or characteristics that appear in their reading.

Go to Print!

Purpose

Authors convey intent through their use of print conventions such as key words, punctuation, bold print, capital letters, and italicized words. Show students how to use these "clues" to help determine what the author thinks is important and to improve their comprehension.

Procedure

Select a poem or a page from a book that demonstrates the use of print conventions. Read through the selection with the class, without discussing print conventions. After reading the selection once, ask students *What ideas is the author trying to convey? What were the most important words or phrases?* Point out the use of print conventions in the text, and explain why authors use them. Have students discuss in small groups why they feel the author used the conventions. Have groups share their findings with the class.

Picture This

Purpose

Good readers identify the meaning of a poem or piece of text and consciously create images in their mind. This process is called visualization. When students picture what is happening in the text and make connections with their own experiences, they improve their comprehension.

Procedure

Select a short poem or piece of text for students to read independently or in pairs. Ask students if they have experienced something similar to the events in the poem or reading selection or have seen television shows or movies that help them visualize the events. Give each student a piece of drawing paper. Have students sketch their visualization.

Prereading Predictor

Purpose

Use a prereading strategy to introduce a short story, poem, novel, or new unit of study. Prereading helps students anticipate what is coming next and actively engages them in the text.

Procedure

Select 15–20 key words or phrases from a reading selection. Write the words or phrases on the chalkboard, and review them with students. Discuss what it means to categorize words. Brainstorm with the class possible categories for the words or phrases. For example, categories might include characters, setting, problem, solution, or parts of speech. Draw a three-column chart on the board. List the categories in the first column. Title the second column *Prereading* and the third column *Postreading*. Ask students to predict which category each word or phrase goes in, and record their responses under "Prereading." Have students read the selection and then provide more specific information for each category based on their reading. Record their responses under "Postreading." Invite students to discuss the differences and similarities between their prereading and postreading answers.

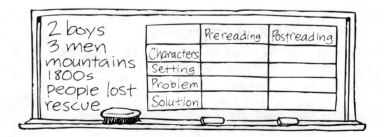

Skim It

Purpose

When the meaning of the text is unclear to students, teach them to go back and skim the text for key words and main ideas. Slower readers can use this strategy to improve their comprehension without getting "bogged down."

Procedure

Select an article, a short piece of text, or a poem. Make an overhead transparency of the selection. Read through the selection once with the class, and demonstrate "skimming" by moving your finger along each line, searching for a specific piece of information. Explain to students that you are rereading parts of the text but not all of it. Have students independently skim a poem or selection for specific vocabulary words, passages, or information. Invite students to share their results with the class.

Stop and Think

Purpose

Use this activity to teach students that good readers think about what they have read and connect newly acquired knowledge to background knowledge. Show students how to synthesize new information, ask questions, visualize, and determine what is important in the text.

Procedure

Select a short story or piece of text for students to read. Have students independently read the first paragraph and think about the topic and important details. Then, have them cover the paragraph with their hand and restate in their own words what they read. Ask students *What is the main idea? What are the important details?* Have them answer the questions aloud and then remove their hand from their paper and check their answers. Encourage students who miss any important details (such as *who, what, where, when, why,* and *how*) to reread the paragraph.

That's Questionable

Purpose

When students generate questions, they become more interested in the reading material and are more likely to better remember the material. This strategy also allows students to clear up any confusing parts and gain new information. Students will find answers in the text, through inferences, or by going to another source.

Procedure

Select a short article or piece of text for students to read independently. Ask students to use sticky notes or a highlighter to mark sections of text where they have questions. Tell them to write explicit questions, such as *When I read _____, it made me wonder about _____*. Have students share their questions with the class, and then record them on a piece of chart paper. Determine which questions can be answered in the text and which questions require students to infer the answer or do further research using another resource. Have students find and write the answers to their questions on a piece of paper.

Through Other Eyes

Purpose

Perspective significantly influences a reader's understanding of text. Guide students through repeated readings of a piece of text to help them discover alternate ways to interpret information when they read from different perspectives.

Procedure

Select a story or an article that presents different perspectives (e.g., male/female, adult/child, or majority/minority) on important concepts and ideas. Have students first independently read the selection to get an overview of the material. Then, ask the class to list different perspectives from the text, and record them on the chalkboard. Model how a person from one of these perspectives would react to the text. Assign each student a perspective to assume as he or she rereads the selection. Discuss the insights students gained by rereading from a different perspective.

What's the Question?

Purpose

Use this strategy to help students actively engage in the reading process with non-fiction text such as textbook material.

Procedure

Select a lesson or chapter from a science, social science, or math textbook. Have students look at the headings, graphics, illustrations, and bold or italicized words as they skim the text. As students skim the text, have them list any questions that come to mind, as well as any unfamiliar vocabulary words. Have them use a dictionary to locate the meaning of the unfamiliar words. Then, ask students to turn each heading and subheading into a question and use graphics and illustrations as ideas for creating questions. After students have generated questions about the text, ask them to read the selection and search for answers to their questions within the text.

Write On

Purpose

When students write about what they read, they are able to reflect on the material and clarify their thinking. Written summaries, questions, and personal responses challenge students to think critically about the text, thereby increasing their comprehension.

Procedure

Select a short piece of text, an article, or a poem for students to read independently. Have students respond to the selection by writing a summary, comparing the selection with their own experiences, or asking questions about the selection. Invite students to share their completed response with the class.

Adjustments

Purpose

We all make adjustments throughout our lives. In the stories students read, characters face changing situations and come to grips with new challenges. A death in the family, a divorce, or a move are situations often faced by story characters and students. This journal activity helps students identify and evaluate an adjustment made by a story character.

Directions

1. Copy a class set of the Adjustments reproducible.

2. Define *adjustment* for the class.

3. Explain that everyone makes adjustments in life and that some are pleasurable and others are painful. Choose a story to read to the class or for students to read independently.

4. After reading the story, brainstorm with the class various types of adjustments people often face, such as changing schools or moving to a new house. Have students think about the adjustments made by the main character in the story. Record student responses on the chalkboard or a piece of chart paper.

5. Give each student a reproducible. Have students describe and illustrate the major adjustments made by the main character. Encourage students to answer the following questions:

   - *Was the adjustment difficult for the character? Why or why not?*
   - *How was the adjustment handled?*
   - *How would you have handled the same situation?*

Extension
Encourage students to do extended readings that will help them deal with life adjustments and then write about their findings in a journal.

Name ______________________ Date ______________

Adjustments

Book Title ______________________________

Author ______________________________

Illustrate and then write about the major adjustments made by the main character.

____

____

____

____

____

____

____

____

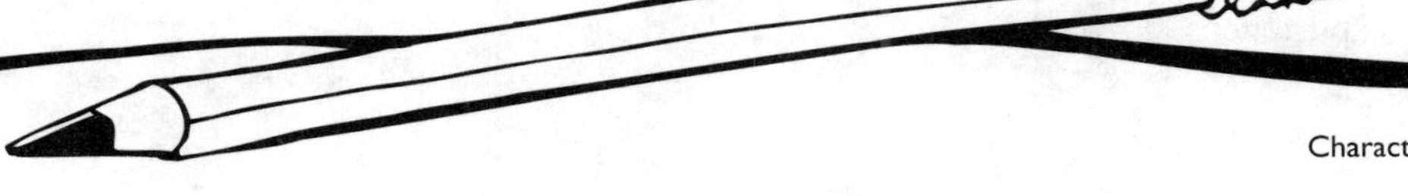

Responding to Literature • 3–6 © 2002 Creative Teaching Press

Before and After

Purpose

Characters aren't static; they grow and change in response to changing circum-stances. In this activity, students chart the development of the main character during the course of the story by describing and illustrating the changes he or she undergoes.

Directions

1 Copy a class set of the Before and After reproducible.

2 Choose a story to read to the class or for students to read independently.

3 After reading the story, discuss with students how important events in life can change people. Have students discuss examples such as moving from grade to grade, deciding that "honesty is the best policy" after being caught cheating on a test, or experiencing an unusually happy or sad event.

4 Brainstorm with the class the life changes the characters in the story went through. Record student responses on the chalkboard or a piece of chart paper.

5 Give each student a reproducible. Have students illustrate the main character's thoughts or actions at the beginning of the story in the "Before" bubble and at the end of the story in the "After" bubble. Then, ask them to write about the main character's thoughts or actions before and after the story, including the changes that occurred.

Extension

Use the Before and After activity to help students learn life lessons through litera-ture. For example, students could read about prejudice in Mildred D. Taylor's *Roll of Thunder, Hear My Cry* (Puffin) or Jeanne Wakatsuki Houston's *Farewell to Manzanar* (Bantam Starfire). Both books provide personal and historical insights into humankind's fragility and show how people come to view life through the lens of their own experiences.

Name _____ Date _____

Before and After

Illustrate and then write about the main character's thoughts or actions before and after the story.

Before

After

Book Title _____ Author _____

_____

_____

_____

_____

Choices! Choices! Choices!

Purpose

The characters in a book face problems and make decisions just as we all do. In analyzing literature, students learn to evaluate the characters' options and decisions. In this activity, students help a character make an important decision. After students review the character's options, have them decide the best way to handle the problem and then compare their decision to that of the character.

Directions

1 Copy a class set of the Choices! Choices! Choices! reproducible.

2 Choose a story to read to the class or for students to read independently.

3 After reading the story, brainstorm with the class the issues that the characters faced. Record student responses on the chalkboard or a piece of chart paper.

4 Give each student a reproducible. Have students describe the issue a character faced in the cloud at the top of the reproducible.

5 Ask students to brainstorm at least three of the character's options, record them on the blank lines, and then list the pros and cons under each option.

6 After students carefully examine the options, have them write at the bottom of the page the decision that they would make in the same situation.

Extension

Have students analyze the choice the main character made. Invite them to take on the role of the character and write three entries in the character's diary that complete the following prompts: *Before I made the decsion, I was thinking . . . After I made the decision, I felt . . . This was a wise or difficult decision because . . .*

Name _____ Date _____

Choices! Choices! Choices!

Book Title _____ Author _____

Describe the issue a character faced and three of the character's options. List the pros and cons of each option. Write the decision you would make in the same situation.

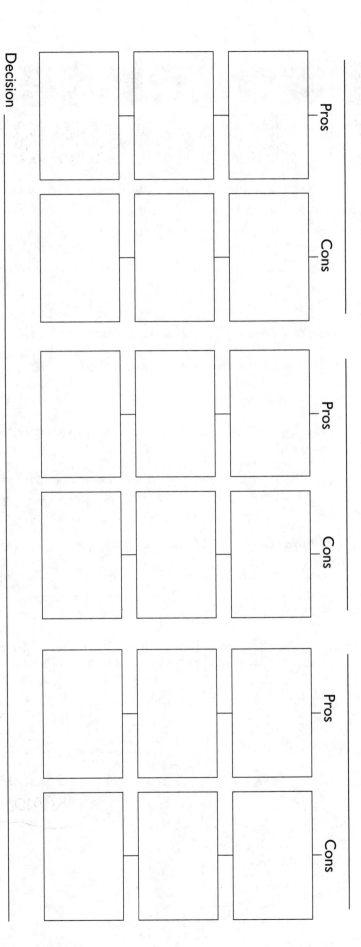

Issue _____

Option One

Pros	Cons

Option Two

Pros	Cons

Option Three

Pros	Cons

Decision _____

Responding to Literature • 3–6 © 2002 Creative Teaching Press

Correspondence

Purpose

When students correspond with a character in a book, the character comes more fully to life. This letter-writing activity gives students the opportunity to reflect on what they have read, ask the characters questions, and give them advice.

Directions

1 Copy a class set of the Correspondence reproducible.

2 Choose a story to read to the class or for students to read independently.

3 After reading the story, ask the class to choose a character to correspond with.

4 Give each student a reproducible. Ask students to write an appropriate date at the top of the page.

5 Tell them to write a letter to the character in which they reflect upon major events in the story, ask questions about how the character feels, and inquire about future events.

6 Have students sign their name at the bottom of the letter.

7 Invite students to write a reply from the character or have a classmate take the role of the character and write a reply.

Extension

Have students write letters from one character to another, from a character in one book to a character in another book, or from a book character to an imagined character. For example, a student could write a letter from Laura in *Little House on the Prairie* by Laura Ingalls Wilder (HarperCollins) to her grandmother in the east. Laura's letter could explain what life is like on the prairie, and her grandmother's letter could tell how much she misses Laura and include questions about prairie life. Also, have students design their own stationery or create a designer stamp. Another excellent model for correspondence is Beverly Cleary's *Dear Mr. Henshaw* (Camelot).

Correspondence

Write a letter to a character. Reflect upon major events, ask questions about how the character feels, and inquire about future events.

Book Title

_____

Author

_____

Date _____

Dear_____,

_____

_____

_____

_____

_____

_____

_____

_____

_____

Sincerely,

_____

Epitaph

Purpose

An epitaph is a message on a tombstone that commemorates the person buried there. In this activity, students write an epitaph for a main character, including a description of the character's impact on family, friends, and the community. Encourage students to use descriptive words, factual information, and interesting anecdotes.

Directions

1. Copy a class set of the Epitaph reproducible.

2. Choose a story to read to the class or for students to read independently.

3. After reading the story, define *epitaph* for the class.

4. Write examples of real or make-believe epitaphs on the chalkboard. Invite the class to discuss the examples.

5. Give each student a reproducible. Discuss the main character of the story, and have students write an epitaph for him or her. The character need not die for students to evaluate the impact of the character on family, friends, and community.

Extension

Have students write epitaphs that reflect different characters' perspectives of the deceased. For example, several barnyard animals could write an epitaph for Charlotte from *Charlotte's Web* by E. B. White (HarperTrophy). Templeton's surly character and Wilbur's sensitive nature would surely result in contrasting epitaphs! Extend the activity by making tombstone models out of cardboard. Have students use paint, crayons, or markers to complete the tombstones. Display the completed tombstones in the classroom.

Name _____   Date _____

Epitaph

Write an epitaph (message) that reflects the impact the character had on family, friends, and the community.

Book Title _____   Author _____

Responding to Literature • 3–6 © 2002 Creative Teaching Press

Job Application

Purpose

Reflecting on a character's strengths and weaknesses gives students the insight to predict how the character will react in different situations. By taking on the character's personality and applying for a job, students make judgments and think critically about the character.

Directions

1 Copy a class set of the Job Application reproducible.

2 Choose a story to read to the class or for students to read independently.

3 After reading the story, brainstorm with the class a list of employment opportunities, vocations studied at school, or jobs mentioned in the book, and discuss the job application process. Record student responses on the chalkboard or a piece of chart paper. Emphasize the importance of correctly filling out forms.

4 Give each student a reproducible. Ask students to take on the personality of a character from the story and reflect on that character's strengths and weaknesses.

5 Help students fill in the basic application data (e.g., name, address, telephone number, social security number, and educational experience). Have students invent information that is not mentioned in the story.

6 Have them record the position for which the character is applying. The job may be mentioned in the story, or it may be purely fictional.

7 Ask students to respond in complete sentences to all questions on the application.

8 Have students review the application, sign and date it, and submit it to the employer (a classmate).

9 Have students evaluate their partner's application and decide if the character is right for the job. Ask students to explain their reasons for hiring or not hiring the applicant and write their reasons on the back of the application.

Extension

Pick up applications for jobs in your community that might be "first job" possibilities for your students (e.g., newspaper carrier, courtesy clerk, cashier, waiter/waitress, gas station attendant, receptionist). Have students reflect on their own strengths and skills and then fill out an application for a job that interests them. Extend this activity by inviting an employer to your class to discuss the qualities he or she looks for in an employee.

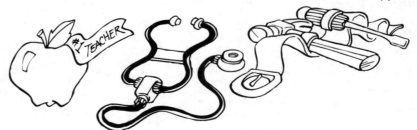

Name _____

Job Application

Fill in the information as if you are a character from the story.

Personal Information

Name	
Address	
Phone Number	Social Security Number

Education History

School Name	Number of Years Completed

Employment Desired

Position Applying For
How did you hear about the job?
Why do you want to work here?

Previous Employment

Employer	How Long?

Why should we hire you?

Signature _____   Date _____

Responding to *Literature* • 3–6 © 2002 Creative Teaching Press

Judges' Panel

Purpose

In this activity, students ask classmates to rate a character based on three qualities and then summarize the results of their survey.

Directions

❶ Copy a class set of the Judges' Panel reproducible.

❷ Choose a story to read to the class or for students to read independently.

❸ After reading the story, brainstorm with the class positive character qualities, such as patience, kindness, goodness, faithfulness, gentleness, and self-control. Record student responses on the chalkboard or a piece of chart paper.

❹ Give each student a reproducible. Have students choose a character to judge.

❺ Ask students to choose three character qualities they would like to use for their "judges' panel" and write them in the spaces provided.

❻ Have students ask nine classmates (three for each character quality) to use the rating scale to judge the character. Tell students to record the judges' names in the boxes and their ratings in the spaces provided.

Extension

Have students list other characters from books as judges and then write ratings from the perspective of the other characters. This makes an excellent cooperative group assignment as it generates a great deal of debate and conversation. Most characters are not all good or all bad. As an alternative, have students brainstorm a list of negative character qualities and rate characters according to these qualities.

❼ Ask students to average the three ratings for each quality and use the information to write a summary of the results.

Judges' Panel

List three character qualities. Show your paper to nine classmates. Record their names in the boxes and their ratings in the spaces below their names. Calculate and record the rating average for each row by adding together the numbers and then dividing the total by 3. Summarize the results.

Rating Scale

10	5	1
Quality demonstrated a great deal	Quality demonstrated occasionally	Quality never demonstrated

Character _____

Book Title _____

Author _____

_____
Character Quality

_____
Rating Average

_____
Character Quality

_____
Rating Average

_____
Character Quality

_____
Rating Average

Summary _____

_____

_____

Responding to Literature • 3–6 © 2002 Creative Teaching Press

Jumping Hurdles

Purpose

Students learn about character development when they identify and analyze a major hurdle faced by a character. A disability, emotional pain, or living conditions will affect how a character deals with situations that arise. In this activity, students describe a hurdle faced by a character and how he or she dealt with it and then make suggestions for overcoming the problem.

Directions

1 Copy a class set of the Jumping Hurdles reproducible.

2 Choose a story to read to the class or for students to read independently.

3 After reading the story, explain to the class that everyone has obstacles to overcome in life (e.g., handicaps or disabilities, emotional pain, a difficult home life). Point out that these hurdles can be difficult to deal with but many people overcome them and enjoy a fulfilling life.

4 Brainstorm with students problems people face, such as peer pressure, competition, illness, handicaps, and prejudice. Record student responses on the chalkboard or a piece of chart paper.

5 Give each student a reproducible. Ask students to complete the reproducible.

6 Have students discuss their answers with a partner.

Extension

Have students write in a journal about a hurdle they are facing in their own lives. Ask them to describe how they are dealing with the problem and possible solutions. If appropriate, hold small-group discussions to have students explore solutions to some of these problems.

Name _____   Date _____

Jumping Hurdles

Book Title _____   Author _____

Answer each question on the lines provided.

What hurdle did your character face?

_____

_____

_____

How did your character deal with this hurdle?

_____

_____

_____

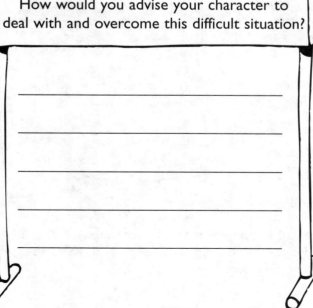

How would you advise your character to deal with and overcome this difficult situation?

_____

_____

_____

Responding to Literature • 3–6 © 2002 Creative Teaching Press

The Life and Times of . . .

Purpose

To fully comprehend an individual's life, it is essential to view the person's growth and development over time, from birth to death. Biographies and autobiographies give readers the opportunity to identify specific experiences that may have helped shape the person's life.

Directions

1 Copy a class set of The Life and Times of . . . reproducible.

2 Choose a story to read to the class or for students to read independently.

3 After reading the story, ask the class to select a person to write a biography about.

4 Give each student a reproducible. Have students divide the person's life into four major periods based on age or major events.

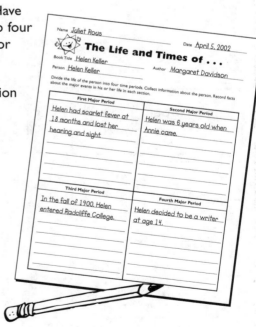

5 Encourage them to gather information about the person's early years and write three or four sentences or phrases under "First Major Period" on the reproducible.

6 Have students list memorable experiences from the person's life under "Second Major Period."

7 Have students list information about any major developments, struggles, or achievements under "Third Major Period."

8 Tell students to list information concerning the person's final years under "Fourth Major Period." Make sure students include some of the reasons why this person will always be remembered.

Extension

Have students use their completed reproducible to write a brief biography or historical fiction story. Invite them to share their biography or story and then display it with an illustration or project of their choice.

Name _____   Date _____

 # The Life and Times of . . .

Book Title _____   Author _____

Person _____

Divide the life of the person into four time periods. Collect information about the person. Record facts about the major events in his or her life in each section.

First Major Period	Second Major Period
_____	_____
_____	_____
_____	_____
_____	_____
_____	_____
_____	_____

Third Major Period	Fourth Major Period
_____	_____
_____	_____
_____	_____
_____	_____
_____	_____

Responding to Literature • 3–6 © 2002 Creative Teaching Press

Performance Review

Purpose

When students read, they analyze the personality traits of a character and classify them as positive or negative. In this activity, students evaluate these traits and justify their ratings.

Directions

1 Copy a class set of the Performance Review reproducible.

2 Choose a story to read to the class or for students to read independently.

3 After reading the story, define personality traits—the behavior a person exhibits—and cluster examples on the chalkboard.

4 Have the class place the traits into positive and negative categories.

5 Give each student a reproducible. Have students choose a character to evaluate.

6 Encourage students to choose six personality traits from the class lists and write them in the first column.

7 Tell students to rate the character on each personality trait using the rating scale explained at the top of the page, or have students design their own grading system.

8 Encourage students to list in the comments column examples from the story that justify their ratings.

Extension

Use this activity as the basis for a character analysis. Have students write a paragraph on each personality trait and add introductory and concluding paragraphs. Have them share their analysis in an oral presentation.

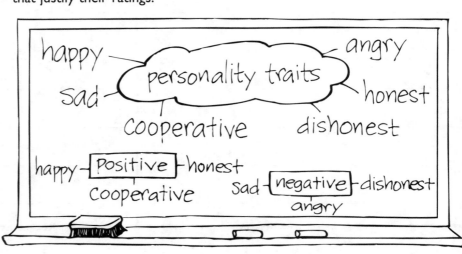

Performance Review

Evaluated by _____   Date _____

Book Title

_____

Author

_____

Character

_____

Rating Scale

| | | | | | | | | | |

10   5   1

Quality   Quality   Quality
demonstrated   demonstrated   never
a great deal   occasionally   demonstrated

List six personality traits in the first column. Rate each of the traits using the rating scale. In the last column, list examples from the story that justify the rating.

Personality Trait	Rating	Comments

Sunny Side/ Stormy Side

Purpose

When students read critically and examine characters in depth, they discover that each character has positive and negative personality traits. Like real people, these characters have a "sunny" and a "stormy" side to their personality. This activity helps students analyze a character's personality traits.

Directions

1 Copy a class set of the Sunny Side/Stormy Side reproducible.

2 Choose a story to read to the class or for students to read independently.

3 After reading the story, explain to the class that characters, like people, are not perfect. Explain that they have both a sunny side (happy, fair, kind) and a stormy side (troubled, grumpy, unkind) to their personality.

4 Give each student a reproducible. Ask students to select a character from a story. Explain that characters with extreme personalities are the most interesting to analyze.

5 Invite students to analyze both sides of their character.

6 Have them list their character's specific personality traits, record an example from the story that illustrates each trait, and list the page number to document each example.

Extension

Have students analyze their own personalities and list both sunny and stormy characteristics. Have them respond to some or all of the following questions in a journal: *Overall, do you have a sunny or a stormy disposition? What has contributed to your overall disposition? How does your disposition affect your relationships? When you feel stormy, what can you do to change that feeling? How can you become a person with a sunnier disposition? What kinds of personalities do your friends have? What type of person do you like to spend time with?*

Name _____   Date _____

Sunny Side/Stormy Side

Book Title _____

Author _____

Character _____

Characters, like people, are not perfect. They both have a sunny side (happy, fair, kind) and a stormy side (troubled, grumpy, unkind) to their personality. Analyze both sides of your character.

Sunny Side			Stormy Side		
Characteristic	Example	Page	Characteristic	Example	Page

Overall, would you say that your character's disposition is sunny or stormy? Explain your answer.

_____

_____

_____

Responding to Literature • 3–6 © 2002 Creative Teaching Press

AQUA Chart

Purpose

In this activity, students list what they **A**lready know about a topic, what **QU**estions they have, and what **A**nswers they think they can find. Have students use the AQUA chart to organize their findings when the class studies a particular subject or reads a favorite nonfiction selection.

Directions

① Copy a class set of the AQUA Chart reproducible.

② Give each student a reproducible. Choose a reading selection or subject topic, and have students write in the **A** section what they already know about the subject.

③ Have students record in the **QU** section the questions they have about the story or topic.

④ Ask them to read the story or research the answers to their questions and then record the answers to their questions in the **A** section at the bottom of the reproducible.

Extension
Invite students to use the AQUA chart to develop their research and outlining skills. Have them complete the first two sections of the chart, transfer their questions onto index cards, and record their answers and sources on the back of the cards. Then, have students organize the index cards into outline form as preparation for writing a report or completing a project.

Name _____   Date _____

AQUA Chart

Book Title or Topic _____

Record below things you already know about the subject and any questions you have. Read your book or research your questions. Write your answers in the last section.

A (Things I **A**lready Know)

QU (**QU**estions I Have)

A (**A**nswers I Found)

Responding to Literature • 3–6 © 2002 Creative Teaching Press

Conflict

Purpose

In all good stories, conflict, a state of disagreement and disharmony, grows out of a connected series of events. In this activity, students identify the conflict in the story and the events that led to it.

Directions

1 Copy a class set of the Conflict reproducible.

2 Choose a story to read to the class or for students to read independently.

3 After reading the story, explain to the class that a conflict is a central part of any good piece of literature. Explain that conflict does not happen overnight; usually there are a series of connected events that lead to a climactic problem. Brainstorm with the class the major events in the story. Record student responses on the chalkboard or a piece of chart paper.

4 Give each student a reproducible. Ask students to list the events in the story that led to the conflict.

5 Have them describe the conflict.

6 Encourage students to predict or prescribe a resolution to the conflict.

7 Ask them to record their suggestions for avoiding the conflict.

Extension

Have students compare two similar historical events. For example, have them compare the Los Angeles riots of 1992 with the Watts riots of 1965. Ask them to identify what was similar or different about the events preceding these two conflicts. Students can also compare historical novels. For example, ask students what similar events led up to the conflicts in *Farewell to Manzanar* by Jeanne Wakatsuki Houston (Bantam Starfire) and *Roll of Thunder, Hear My Cry* by Mildred D. Taylor (Puffin). Have students brainstorm a list of intervention techniques that could prevent these problems from escalating into major conflicts.

Name _____   Date _____

Conflict

Book Title _____

Author _____

List the events that led to the conflict in your story.

First, _____

_____

Then, _____

_____

Then, _____

_____

Now, _____

_____

Describe the conflict. _____

_____

Predict or prescribe a resolution to your character's conflict. _____

_____

What event(s) would you change in the story to avoid the conflict described above? _____

_____

Responding to Literature • 3–6 © 2002 Creative Teaching Press

Let's Celebrate

Purpose

A birthday, a homecoming, a wedding—are all occasions for celebration. In this activity, students identify and describe a cause for celebration from a story and then prepare an invitation so that everyone can join in the fun.

Directions

1 Copy a class set of the Let's Celebrate reproducible.

2 Choose a story that includes a cause for celebration to read to the class or for students to read independently.

3 After reading the story, discuss with students the cause for celebration. Ask the class to select the guest of honor.

4 Give each student a reproducible. Have students describe the cause for celebration and list the appropriate time, date, and place.

5 Ask them to select the host or hostess of the party. It can be another character from the story or the student.

6 Invite students to fold the invitation and decorate the cover.

7 Display the completed invitations throughout the classroom.

Extension

Have students write about a time in their lives when they had a reason to celebrate. Focus on celebrations that mark the solution to a problem, such as the end of a serious illness, the recovery of a family member from an accident, the end of a long period of unemployment, or a personal achievement such as making a sports team or earning a good grade in school. Have students compare and contrast their experiences with those of the story characters.

Name _____   Date _____

Let's Celebrate

Guest(s) of Honor: _____

_____

We're celebrating because _____

_____

Date: _____

Time: _____

Place: _____

Hosted by: _____

_____

Hope to see you!

Responding to Literature • 3–6 © 2002 Creative Teaching Press

News Flash!

Purpose

Newspaper articles present factual information in a concise manner. The first paragraph or two answers the questions *who, what, when, where, why,* and *how.* In this activity, students write a newspaper article that summarizes a major event from a story.

Directions

1 Copy a class set of the Daily News reproducible.

2 Choose a story to read to the class or for students to read independently.

3 Bring the local newspaper to class. After reading the story, read aloud several short articles of interest. Point out that the articles begin by answering the questions *who, what, when, where, why,* and *how.*

4 Give each student a reproducible. Invite students to write their own article that summarizes the main event(s) of the story and answers the questions *who, what, when, where, why,* and *how.*

5 Have students give their article a title that summarizes the main event.

6 Tell them to record their name on the byline and the date and place of origin on the dateline.

7 Encourage students to illustrate their article in the box.

Extension

When students have successfully summarized the main events of the story, ask them to consider their report from another perspective. Have them write an article from the perspective of the main character and compare and contrast it with the first article. *The True Story of the 3 Little Pigs* by Jon Scieszka (Puffin) provides a prime example of how perspective can influence the description of a person.

Name _____ Date _____

Today's Weather

Daily News

25¢

Write an article that summarize the main event(s) of the story and answers the questions *who, what, when, where, why,* and *how.*

Book Title _____ Author _____

Title of article _____

Byline _____

Dateline _____

_____

_____

_____

_____

_____

_____

_____

_____

_____

_____

_____

_____

_____

_____

Reading Log

Purpose

A reading log is a great way for students to keep a record of independent reading. It helps students to identify main ideas and frame their responses to the books they are reading. Reading logs are also excellent tools for teachers, letting them see at a glance whether students comprehend the material they read independently.

Directions

1 Copy a class set of the Reading Log reproducible.

2 Choose a story to read to the class or for students to read independently.

3 Give each student a reproducible before he or she begins to read.

4 After each chapter or reading period, have students record the date, the pages read, new vocabulary, a summary of the main events, and their feelings about the reading material.

5 Have students keep a reading log for the whole book. Periodically discuss new vocabulary, main events, and student feelings.

Extension

Have students use their reading logs to aid them in rewriting their favorite book for younger students. Have them retell and illustrate the main events in a Big Book or mini-book format. Invite younger students to your classroom, and have students share their stories with a small group.

Reading Log

Name _____

Book Title _____

Author _____

Record the date, pages read, new vocabulary, a summary of the main events, and your feelings about the reading material.

Date	Pages	Vocabulary	Summary/Feelings

Responding to Literature • 3–6 © 2002 Creative Teaching Press

Story Map

Purpose

Story maps are a fun way for students to retell a story. They also help you assess students' ability to identify the main actions in the plot that move the story towards its resolution. In this activity, students sequence events in their reading and writing.

Directions

1 Copy a class set of the Story Map reproducible.

2 Choose a story to read to the class or for students to read independently.

3 After reading the story, brainstorm with the class the characters and main events. Record student responses on the chalkboard or a piece of chart paper.

4 Give each student a reproducible. Have students list the main characters in the middle of the page.

5 Invite students to work in small groups, individually, or as a class. Help students identify the main events. Have them write about and illustrate each event.

Extension

To help students create stories of their own, it is essential for them to see the sequence of events generated by the action and development of events in the story. After using the reproducible with stories read in class, ask students to use it to plan their own compositions. After students identify the main actions in the plot, it will be easier for them to write their stories.

Event 1

Willy's grandfather became very ill.

Name _____   Date _____

Story Map

Book Title _____   Author _____

Setting _____

List the main characters. Chart the story by writing about and illustrating each main event.

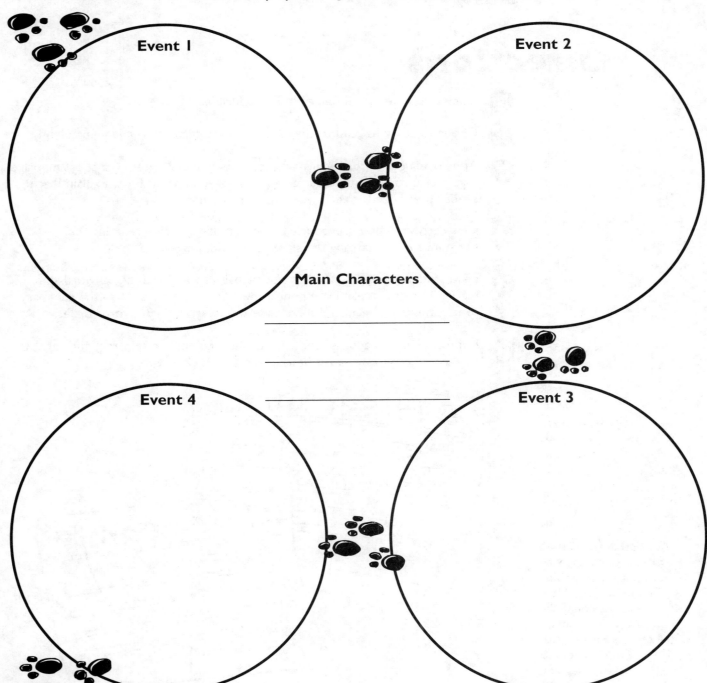

Event 1

Event 2

Main Characters

_____

_____

_____

Event 4

Event 3

Responding to Literature • 3–6 © 2002 Creative Teaching Press

Telegram

Purpose

It is often difficult for students to identify and summarize the main points of a story. In this activity, students practice this essential skill by producing a "telegram summary" of a story.

Directions

1 Copy a class set of the Telegram reproducible.

2 Choose a story to read to the class or for students to read independently.

3 After reading the story, explain to students that a telegram is a short message that is electronically transmitted and delivered in paper form. Explain that the sender pays a fee for each word he or she sends.

4 Give each student a reproducible. Have students begin preparing their telegram by summarizing the story they read in 50 words or less.

5 Have students work in small groups or pairs to evaluate the 50-word summaries. Have them eliminate nonessential words to scale down the summary to its essential aspects and then write the telegram in 30 words or less.

6 Invite students to address and cut out their completed telegram and send it to another classroom, a fictitious address, or a classmate.

Extension

Extend this activity by assigning a dollar value to each word. Have students count the words in their summary and calculate how much it will cost them to send their telegram.

Name _____ Date _____

Telegram

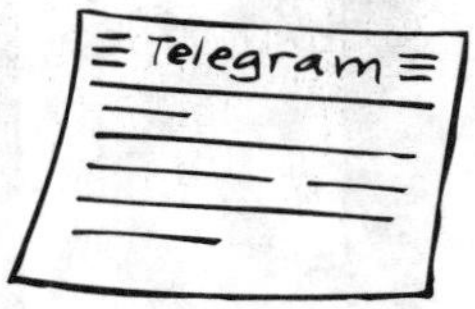

Book Title _____ Author _____

Begin preparing your telegram by summarizing, in 50 words or less, the most essential aspects of the story.

_____

_____

_____

_____

_____

_____

Write your telegram below using 30 words or less. Remember, you will pay a fee for each word you use.

Telegram

Send the following message:

To _____ Phone Number _____

Address _____

City & State _____ Zip Code _____

_____

_____

_____

_____

Sender's Name _____ Phone Number _____

Responding to Literature • 3–6 © 2002 Creative Teaching Press

Hollywood, Here We Come!

Purpose

Lights! Camera! Action! This activity is designed to challenge students to outline the major scenes, characters, and props needed to dramatize a story.

Directions

1 Copy a class set of the Hollywood, Here We Come! reproducible.

2 Choose a story to read to the class or for students to read independently.

3 After reading the story, ask students what the major scenes, characters, and props would be if they were to turn the story into a movie. Help students divide the book into the major scenes based on chapter headings or major events. Record student responses on the chalkboard or a piece of chart paper.

4 Brainstorm with the class the props needed for each scene.

5 Give each student a reproducible. Have students list the major scenes, characters and props needed for each scene.

Extension

After students have completed the reproducible, have them work in cooperative groups to write a script for one or more scenes. Have the whole class combine the scenes to create a complete screenplay. Student-authored productions are big hits with parents and students alike and make fabulous Back-to-School Night or Open House productions. Videotape the production if possible.

Book Title
By the Great Horn Spoon
Author
Sid Fleischman

Name _____   Date _____

Hollywood, Here We Come!

Book Title _____   Author _____

Think about how you could turn this story into a movie. List the major scenes and the characters and props needed for each scene.

Scenes	Characters	Props

Responding to Literature • 3–6 © 2002 Creative Teaching Press

Snapshot

Purpose

The setting of the story describes where and when the story takes place. The author's description and the story's illustrations help readers visualize the setting. Have students recreate their favorite setting by taking a "snapshot" and sharing it with their classmates.

Directions

1 Copy a class set of the Snapshot reproducible.

2 Choose a story to read to the class or for students to read independently.

3 After reading the story, brainstorm with students the setting described in the story. Record student responses on the chalkboard or a piece of chart paper.

4 Give each student a reproducible. Have students illustrate the setting in the picture frame, including any specific details described in the story. Students can also draw characters.

5 Ask students to record the date and place of the snapshot.

6 Encourage students to describe their snapshot. Remind them to use adjectives and adverbs to give the reader a clear picture of the scene.

Extension
Extend the activity by compiling the snapshots into a class photo album. Cover two pieces of cardboard with contact paper. Hole-punch the student snapshots and cardboard. Bind the book with string or yarn.

Name _____   Date _____

Snapshot

Book Title _____   Author _____

Illustrate the setting. Include any specific details described in the story. Write a description of the setting below your drawing.

Date of Photograph _____   Place _____

Description _____

_____

_____

_____

_____

_____

_____

Responding to Literature • 3–6 © 2002 Creative Teaching Press

Travel Brochure

Purpose

Characters often have a hideaway or a place of refuge from the problems that beset them. They may seek refuge in a world of fantasy or imagination, or they may have a secret place to which they can escape. Have students identify and describe a character's place of refuge and let others experience the setting by creating a travel brochure for it.

Directions

1 Copy a class set of the Travel Brochure reproducible. Gather travel brochures from local travel agencies.

2 Choose a story to read to the class or for students to read independently.

3 After reading the story, brainstorm with the class the definition of *hideaway*. Ask students *What makes a good hideaway?* Record student responses on the chalkboard or a piece of chart paper.

4 Share the travel brochures with students. Point out the colorful language and enticing illustrations. Remind students that travel brochures make a particular destination very inviting.

5 Give each student a reproducible. Show students how to fold their reproducible into thirds.

6 Have students create a beautiful picture of the destination (hideaway) on the front cover and write the title of the book.

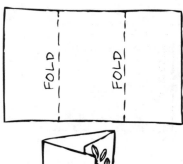

7 Invite students to describe the main character's hideaway, including physical features, location, and interesting anecdotes to entice the reader, and draw a picture of it in the 1st column.

8 Invite students to explain why the hideaway is the best place and draw a picture to support their opinion in the 2nd column.

9 Have students explain what makes the hideaway extra special and draw a picture to illustrate their opinion in the 3rd column.

Extension

Have students choose a place of refuge for themselves and plan to spend 15 minutes a day there for five consecutive days. Have them record their thoughts in a personal journal. Inspire their writing by posing the following questions: *How does it feel to have a place of refuge? Do you think a place of refuge is important in a person's life? Explain your answer. How can having a place to go to make your life more exciting?*

Name _____

Date _____

Everyone needs a place to get away to,
a place where they can think and relax.

This is the place!

Describe the main character's hideaway.

_____
_____
_____
_____
_____

Illustration

Describe why it is the best hideaway.

_____
_____
_____
_____
_____

Illustration

Describe the extra special features.

_____
_____
_____
_____
_____

Illustration

Resounding Words

Purpose

Descriptive writing is full of onomatopoeic words—words that imitate sounds. In this activity, students increase their awareness of onomatopoeic words by identifying them in a story.

Directions

1 Copy a class set of the Resounding Words reproducible.

2 Choose a story that uses onomatopoeia to read to the class or for students to read independently.

3 After reading the story, define *onomatopoeia* (i.e., to name a thing or an action by the verbal imitation of the sound associated with it) for the class.

4 Brainstorm with the class examples of onomatopoeic words such as *whiz, boom, bang, ring,* and *clang.* Record student responses on the chalkboard or a piece of chart paper.

5 Give each student a reproducible. Have students describe in the left column the source of the sounds found throughout the story.

6 Ask students to write in the right column the onomatopoeic words used to describe the sounds.

Extension

Ask students to write a paragraph describing a robot walking through a house without onomatopoeic words. Then, have them write the same paragraph using onomatopoeic words. Invite students to read aloud both paragraphs and explain which paragraph is more effective and why. To extend this activity, have them write a full-length story or comic strip using lively onomatopoeic language. Encourage students to use existing onomatopoeic words or create their own.

Name _____   Date _____

 # Resounding Words

Book Title _____   Author _____

Describe in the left column the source of the sounds found throughout the story. In the right column, write the onomatopoeic words used to describe the sounds.

Source of Sound	Examples of Onomatopoeia (words that imitate sounds)

Similes and Metaphors

Purpose

Good writing is enlivened by figurative language like similes and metaphors. This activity challenges students to locate these figures of speech in a favorite book passage and identify the two objects of comparison.

Directions

1 Copy a class set of the Similes and Metaphors reproducible.

2 Define for the class the terms *simile* and *metaphor* as figurative language where two objects are being compared. Explain that a simile uses the terms "as" or "like" in the comparison while a metaphor does not. Provide a few examples, and have students brainstorm additional examples. Record the similes and metaphors on the chalkboard or a piece of chart paper.

3 Give each student a reproducible. Choose a story to read to the class or for students to read independently. As students read the story or selected passage, have them record examples of similes and metaphors in the left column.

4 After students complete the reading, ask them to go back and identify the two objects being compared in each figure of speech and list each pair in the right column.

5 Have students choose their favorite simile or metaphor to illustrate.

6 Discuss with the class how these "word pictures" add a visualization of the comparison.

Extension

Have students enrich their own writing with the use of similes and metaphors and draw illustrations to accompany their stories. Compile the completed projects in a class book for all to enjoy.

Similes
- Justin was as fast as lightning.
- Missy has cheeks like roses.
- Liza jumped like a kangaroo.

Metaphors
- Rob's a sly fox.
- Maddy's a shining star in math.
- He's a diamond in the rough.

Name _____ Date _____

 Greg is a shining star.

Similes and Metaphors

Book Title _____ Author _____

Record examples of similes and metaphors from the story in the left column. For each example, identify the two objects being compared in the right column. Illustrate your favorite simile or metaphor.

Similes and Metaphors	Comparison

Illustration

Responding to Literature • 3–6 © 2002 Creative Teaching Press

Word Collector

Purpose

Literature is filled with words and expressions from other cultures. This activity is designed to enrich students' vocabulary by having them record unusual words or expressions and the interpretation of the words.

Directions

1 Copy a class set of the Word Collector reproducible.

2 Choose a story to read to the class or for students to read independently.

3 Give each student a reproducible. Have students label the left column with the name of the country where the phrase originated and then label the right column with their own country.

4 When students come across an unfamiliar expression or a word typical of the country being studied, have them record this word or expression and its interpretation on their chart.

Extension

Extend this vocabulary activity to include a study of colloquialisms, dialects, and syntax. This type of study helps students understand and appreciate different language backgrounds. *Mirandy and Brother Wind* by Patricia McKissack (Dragonfly Books) provides an excellent example of black dialect. Students instinctively understand the characters' speech through contextual clues. Have students record their findings under two columns.

Name _____ Date _____

Word Collector

Book Title _____ Author _____

Record unfamiliar words or expressions typical of the specific country you are reading about.

Country of Origin	**My Country**
_____	_____

Book Comparison

Purpose

Sharpen students' higher-level thinking skills by asking them to compare and contrast two works of literature related by genre, theme, plot, style, or characterization.

Directions

1 Copy a class set of the Book Comparison reproducible.

2 Choose two stories to read to the class or for students to read independently.

3 After reading both stories, give each student a reproducible. Have students record the names of the two stories.

4 Have students work in small groups to brainstorm similarities and differences between the two stories. Have students record their findings on the reproducible.

5 Ask students which book was their favorite and why. Encourage them to be specific and give at least three reasons in support of their choice.

Extension
Use a traditional Venn diagram to extend this activity. Have students record similarities where the circles overlap and differences where they do not.

Both books are based on true stories.

The Reeds traveled farther west than the Ingalls.

Little House on the Prairie

Patty Reed's Doll
The Story of the Donner Party

Name _____   Date _____

Book Comparison

Book Title _____

Book Title _____

Record similarities and differences between the two books.

Similarities	Differences

My favorite book was _____

I liked it because _____

_____

Responding to Literature • 3–6 © 2002 Creative Teaching Press

Other Perspectives

Purpose

Often, an event is seen quite differently by the people involved. Each person, quite naturally, sees the event from his or her perspective. After reading a story, have students choose an event in the story and look at it from different points of view.

Directions

1 Copy a class set of the Other Perspectives reproducible.

2 Choose a story to read to the class or for students to read independently.

3 After reading the story, brainstorm with the class a list of interesting events in the novel. Record student responses on the chalkboard or a piece of chart paper.

4 Give each student a reproducible. Have students choose one event from the list and record it in the scroll.

5 Ask students to choose four characters from the story and record each character's name and his or her perception of the event in a separate box.

Extension
Have students use the reproducible to analyze an event in their own life. Encourage them to look at the event from their point of view and from that of their parents, teachers, friends, and siblings.

Name _____ Date _____

Other Perspectives

Book Title _____ Author _____

Often, an event is seen in different ways by those involved. Choose an event from your story and look at it from different perspectives. Record the event and each character's name and his or her perception of the event in the boxes below.

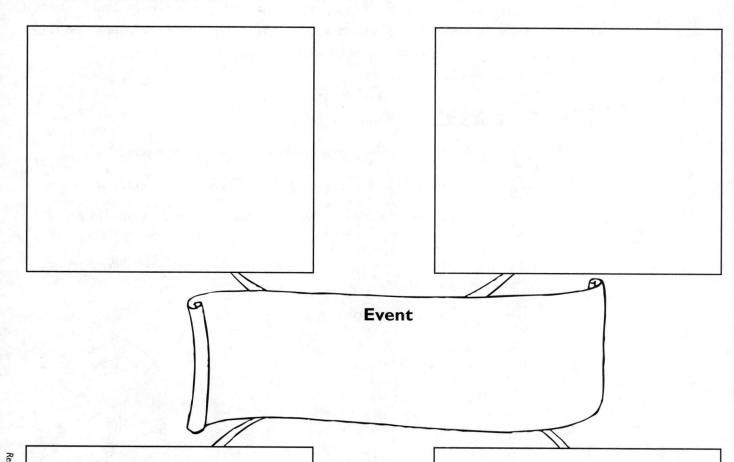

Event

Responding to Literature • 3–6 © 2002 Creative Teaching Press

Three-Way Venn Diagram

Purpose

Call upon students to think critically. Have them compare and contrast three works of literature related by genre, theme, plot, style, authorship, or characterization. They may choose novels, short stories, poems, plays, or films.

Directions

1 Copy a class set of the Three-Way Venn Diagram reproducible.

2 Choose three familiar books for students to compare and contrast.

3 Give each student a reproducible. Have students record the titles of the books.

4 Tell students to list similarities where the circles overlap and differences where they do not.

5 As a class, complete a circle of the diagram together.

6 Encourage students to complete the rest of the diagram independently or in cooperative groups.

Extension

Use the three-way Venn diagram as the basis for a comparative essay. Have students use the information in each of the seven sections of the Venn diagram to write a separate paragraph for the body of the essay. Have students complete the essay by adding an introductory and a concluding paragraph. This activity is ideal for the student who finds linear outlining cumbersome.

Brazilian rain forest paintings

a man falls asleep and the rain forest creature visits him

a man is thinking about deforestation

erosion
sloth
monkeys

birds
people
concern for future

collage illustrations

Australian rain forest

a boy and his father

ends with a question

watercolor illustrations

the tall trees guard the animals of the rain forest when the flood comes

Three-Way Venn Diagram

Record similarities and differences among the three books.

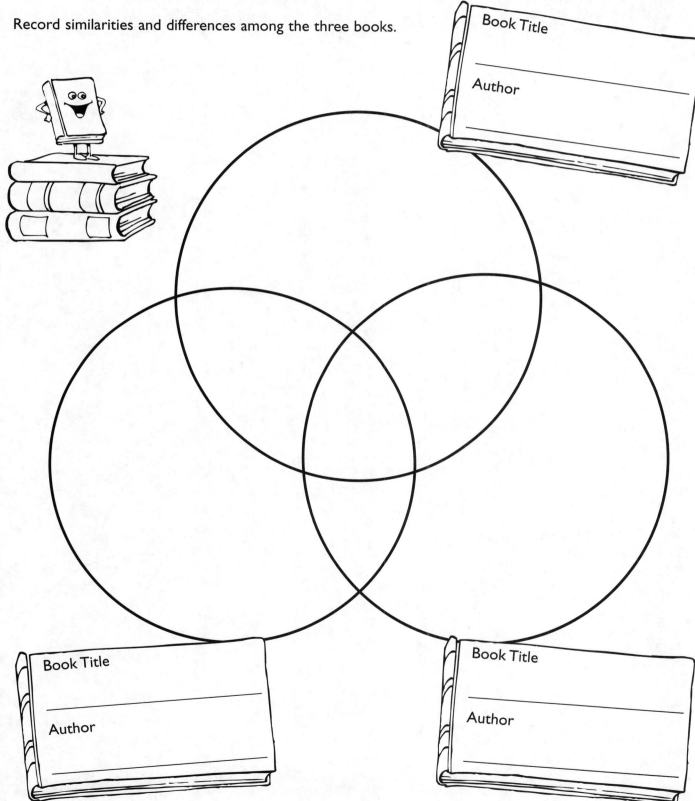

Book Title
_____
Author
_____

Book Title
_____
Author
_____

Book Title
_____
Author
_____

Responding to Literature • 3–6 © 2002 Creative Teaching Press